Samuel
Prophet and Judge

RICHIE WHALEY • ILLUSTRATED BY **DEAN SHELTON**

BROADMAN PRESS
Nashville, Tennessee

Dewey Decimal Classification: J221.92
Subject heading: SAMUEL
Printed in the United States of America

Contents

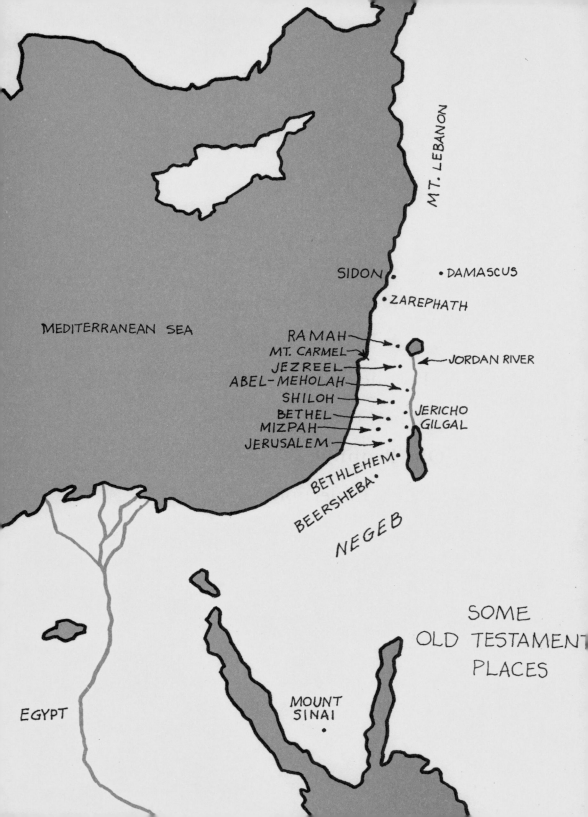

MT. LEBANON

SIDON •   • DAMASCUS

• ZAREPHATH

MEDITERRANEAN   SEA

RAMAH
MT. CARMEL
JEZREEL   ← JORDAN RIVER
ABEL-MEHOLAH
SHILOH
BETHEL   • JERICHO
MIZPAH   GILGAL
JERUSALEM

BETHLEHEM •
BEERSHEBA •

NEGEB

EGYPT

MOUNT
SINAI •

SOME
OLD TESTAMENT
PLACES

A Special Child

A special little boy came to the beautiful tent house of God in Shiloh. This boy was going to live in God's house, not just on God's day, but every day and every night.

But this is not what made Samuel special. In that long-ago time, other boys grew up in God's house. They were the sons of God's priests, who lived in the place of worship and took care of it.

What made Samuel special was that he was not a priest's son. His real home was Ramah, in the hills a few miles from Shiloh.

Samuel's father—Elkanah—loved his family dearly. Once there had been much quarreling and sadness in Elkanah's home, but not anymore—and all because of Samuel.

Let's start at the beginning. Elkanah had two wives. One wife had children, but the other did not. The wife who had no children was Hannah. She was sad, for she wanted children very much.

Hannah was especially sad one time when the family went to Shiloh to worship. After worship the family had a feast. Hannah was so sad that she did not even eat.

Instead, Hannah went into the place of prayer. She cried as she prayed for a baby. "God," she begged, "if you will give me a son, I promise to lend him to you forever."

Eli the priest sat by the door, watching. Hannah's lips were moving, but no sounds came from them. Eli thought Hannah was drunk and said to her, "Shame on you, being drunk, especially here!"

"But I am not drunk," Hannah said. And she told Eli about her prayer. Eli told her not to worry; God would answer her prayer. Hannah believed Eli and was no

7

longer sad. She even ate.

Eli was right. God did answer Hannah's prayer. The next year she did have a son and called him Samuel. It means "I have asked the Lord for him."

Hannah loved her son very much. She taught him to help, and she must have talked with him often about God.

Hannah did not forget her promise. When Samuel was about three years old, the whole family went to the tabernacle. They carried gifts for Eli and special offerings for worshiping God.

Proudly, Hannah took her son to the old priest. "You probably don't remember me," she said. "I am the woman you saw praying for a child. God heard my prayer. Here is the son he sent to me."

Hannah gently set the child Samuel before Eli. "I promised to lend him to God, and I am willing to keep that promise. He belongs to God for as long as he lives."

9

Then, Hannah sang praises to God, saying:

"God has made me glad!
He knows us.
He cares for us.
He knows what is best.
God is great!"

Elkanah and all his family—except Samuel—went back home to Ramah. Samuel stayed in Shiloh to help Eli and serve God.

Thinkback: What made Samuel a special child? Was it because his father was rich? because he got to make an exciting trip? Why, then? How was Hannah a good mother?

A Boy Who Obeyed God

Samuel's parents came to visit him at least once every year. And, each year Hannah brought him a new linen robe she had woven.

You see, a child who was lent to God wore special clothes. One short piece was called an ephod. It was like a loose vest with shoulder straps and was tied with a special belt. Under the ephod Samuel wore a linen coat or robe that reached to

11

12

his feet. It was this robe that Hannah made and brought to Samuel each year.

What did a boy do in Shiloh? Eli and other priests taught Samuel to read and to write. They helped him learn God's laws. Samuel learned to say many parts of the law without even looking at the words. He learned that God wants his people to obey him.

Like other boys in those days, Samuel listened to true stories of long ago. He heard tales of brave men and women who listened to God and tried to serve him.

But, living in Shiloh was not all listening to exciting tales of long ago! Samuel had work to do in the tent of worship. He spent much of his time helping Eli. He cleaned the bowls and lamps that were used in worship. He rubbed them till they shone.

At night Samuel slept near a special golden box. It was the ark of the covenant. Inside were special treasures. One treasure was a copy of the Ten Commandments.

Eli was good and kind. But his two

grown sons were very spoiled. They were supposed to help people worship. Instead, they made fun of the worship of God.

Eli's sons were also greedy. People who came to worship God were glad to share their meat with the priests. But Eli's sons sent servants to grab the best part of the meat.

Eli said to his sons: "Shame on you. You must stop. What you are doing is against God's law."

But they paid no attention.

A messenger from God warned Eli about his sons: "Why do you let them rob the people? Why do you let them make a wicked game out of my rules for worship? If you do not stop them, I must punish all of you!"

Still, nothing changed.

Then, one night all was quiet. Eli was sound asleep in his room. Samuel was asleep, too.

Suddenly a voice spoke Samuel's name!

"Yes, sir," answered Samuel, and ran to

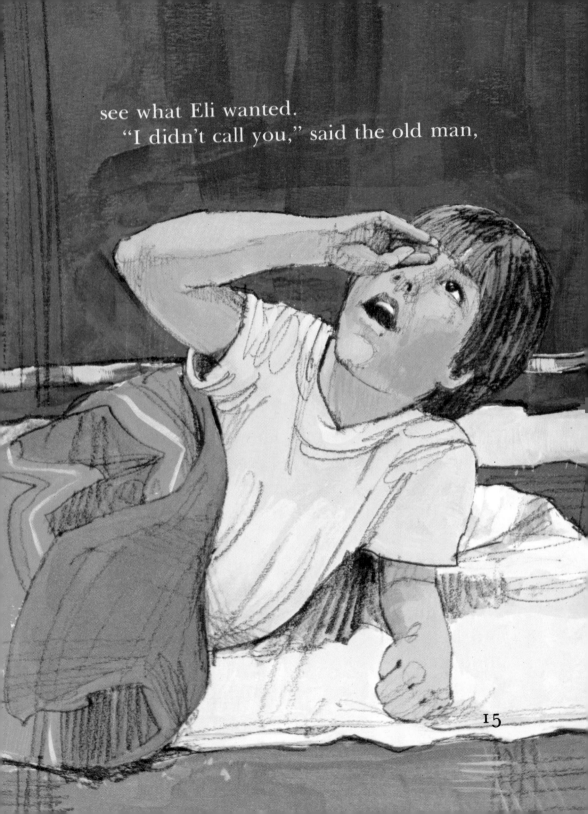

see what Eli wanted.

"I didn't call you," said the old man,

15

sleepily. "Go back to bed." And Samuel returned to his sleeping mat.

The same thing happened a second time—and a third. Each time Samuel got up and went to Eli, saying, "You called me, and here I am."

The third time Eli knew whose voice Samuel had heard. "Go back to bed," he said again, but he added, "If the voice calls again, answer this way: Speak to me, Lord. I am your servant. I am listening."

Samuel did as Eli said. And the voice of God gave him a sad message: "Someday I must punish Eli and his family for the wickedness of his sons. They have refused to obey me and my laws. And Eli has not stopped them. Now it is too late."

The next morning Eli said, "Samuel, tell me what God said to you last night."

It was very hard for Samuel to obey, but he did. He told the truth, exactly.

As young Samuel grew, he pleased God and he pleased others. He grew to be a good man. People knew that God was with Samuel. And they listened to what Samuel said about God.

Thinkback: What do you think Samuel would have said when his parents asked, "What have you been doing at the tabernacle?"

A Faithful Judge

"What shall we do?" said the leaders of God's people, Israel. "The Philistines keep killing our people and taking our land. If we carry God's treasure box into battle, we will surely win."

They acted as if God was inside the box called the ark of the covenant. They thought it would bring them luck.

And so, a message came to the tent of worship, "Send the ark, and we shall win."

Eli's sons did not try to help people understand that God is everywhere, not in a box. They went back to the battle with the ark, which was against God's law.

The enemy fought even harder. Again they won. God's people tried to escape, but many were killed. Two of those killed were Eli's sons. Even worse, the Philistines captured the ark!

A messenger brought the bad news to Shiloh. When blind old Eli heard it, he fell from his seat and broke his neck.

Great sadness was over the land. Eli was dead. And the beautiful tent of worship had to be taken down and hidden away.

The Philistines thought they had captured God when they took the ark. "Now," they said, "the great God will have to fight for us!"

God showed the Philistines how wrong they were. For seven months terrible things happened in their land. "What have we done?" they cried. Finally, they decided to send the ark back to God's people.

Carefully, they set the ark on a new cart, pulled by two cows. Beside the ark, they set five fine gifts of gold. Straight down the road went the cows—as if God

was guiding them—straight back to Israel.

What was Samuel doing all this time? He was doing what God told him to do. He was serving as a good and fair judge, helping people settle their quarrels. But Samuel was sad. Everywhere he saw God's people copying the ways of their wicked neighbors. They even began to worship idols.

Again and again, Samuel said: "You are disobeying God. You are to worship him only!"

At first, people would not listen. Then, when trouble came they began to wish for God's help. Samuel's message was:

"Do you really want God to be your

21

God? Then, be sorry and turn from your evil ways. Get rid of these idols. Worship God and obey him only. Then he can help you."

This time the people did as Samuel asked. He said: "Meet me at Mizpah. There I shall pray to God for you."

The people had come to Mizpah before. There, many times Samuel, the fair judge, had settled their quarrels. This time he helped them worship God. God's people, Israel, told God they were sorry for disobeying. And Samuel was glad.

Someone else came to Mizpah that day—the enemy! Five Philistine kings thought it would be a good place to win another battle against Israel.

When God's people learned that the big army was nearby, they were afraid. "Keep praying for us," they begged Samuel. And Samuel did.

God answered quickly. Suddenly, thunder rolled and crashed from the skies. The Philistines were frightened and began to run.

23

Quickly and bravely, God's people marched from Mizpah. They were no longer afraid. They knew God! That day for the first time in many years, Israel won a great victory. It would last a long, long time!

Samuel knew—and so did the people—who had really won that day. And so, Samuel set up a marker near Mizpah. He gave it a name: Stone of Help.

"Remember this day," he said. "Remember it was God who helped us all the way."

Thinkback: What was the biggest mistake God's people made? What is the difference between luck and God's help?

Can you remember a time of trouble when God helped you? How did you thank him?

Which of these words describe Samuel as a judge? Can you tell why you choose each word?

brave famous patient good kind proud

The Prophet-Judge Finds a King

Peace came to the land. Samuel kept doing what God had chosen him to do. He went from town to town, teaching and judging the people fairly.

Soon there was more teaching than Samuel could do alone. He began special schools. There he taught young men whom God had chosen also. From Samuel they learned how to show the people God's ways.

25

You would think God's people would be happy. But they were not. They looked at other nations around them. Everyone else had a king. People of Israel began to want a king, too. So they came to Samuel. "We want to be like other nations. Choose a king for us," the people said.

This was a new problem for Samuel to judge. He prayed to God about it, and God said: "Do not have hurt feelings. They are not against you. They are against me. They have forgotten all I have done for them. Tell them what will happen when they have a king."

"A king will treat you like slaves," Samuel told the people. "Your children will have to be his soldiers and his servants. He will take your best land and best crops. Once you choose to have a king, you cannot change your mind."

"Give us a king anyway!" the people cried.

Samuel told God, and God's answer was quick, "Tell them they shall have what they want—a king!"

One day after all the people had gone home, God spoke to Samuel: "Tomorrow a man will come to you. He comes because I want him to. On his head pour the oil used to honor kings."

It happened exactly as God had said. Samuel was on his way to worship. Coming toward him were two men. One was Saul—handsome and tall. To Samuel God said: "This is the man. He will rule."

27

Then Saul asked, "Where does the seer live?" (*Seer* was the word for a good man who could tell things that would come true someday. God's messengers, the prophets, were seers, too.)

Samuel replied: "I am the one you are looking for. Come worship with me. Then eat with me. I have something important to tell you. Tomorrow I will answer all your questions, and you can leave."

Saul was puzzled, but he did as Samuel asked. Samuel gave a great feast. Saul sat at the best place. His was the best part of the meat. That night Saul slept on a special bed on the flat roof.

Early the next day, Samuel walked to the edge of town with Saul and his servant. "Saul," he said, "tell your servant to go ahead. I must tell you what God has said."

When they were alone, Samuel took a jar of olive oil from his robe. He anointed Saul's head and kissed him, the way a king was honored in those days.

Then Samuel said: "God has chosen

you to rule his people. So that you will know I tell the truth, I shall tell you exactly what will happen as you go home. Remember, God will be with you, whatever happens."

And again it all happened exactly as Samuel had said. People wondered why Saul seemed so different. He told everything that happened—except what Samuel had said about his becoming king.

What did Samuel do next? He called God's people to worship at Mizpah. There he said to them: "You have asked for a king. You shall have your king."

Samuel told the people to group by tribes. From the tribe of Benjamin, the smallest of all, he called for Saul.

No one answered. People asked, "Could there be a mistake?"

God answered: "There is no mistake. Saul is hiding in the supplies." And that is where the people found him.

"Here is your king!" Samuel announced. "God has chosen Saul to be your ruler."

30

"Long live the king!" the people shouted.

Then Samuel told how God wanted his king to act. All his words were written in a book and put in a special place.

Thinkback: Why did God let the people have their way? Who chose Saul to be king?

31

When the King Failed

It was a happy day—a day of
celebration. Everyone was praising the
new king, Saul. He had just won a battle
against an enemy king.

Samuel was not jealous. He was glad the
people loved their new king. He just
wanted them to remember God's words.

"You must love God most of all," he

33

warned. "If you turn against God's ways, you will be punished. Obey God and serve him. I shall always pray for you and give you God's message."

Saul started out as a good king. At first he listened to Samuel, as God had said. When Saul wanted to drive the enemy from the land, Samuel gave him a plan.

After seven days Saul's troops were to gather at Gilgal. Samuel would meet them there, make an offering to God, and pray for his help. Then the battle would start.

The seventh day came, and there was no sign of Samuel. King Saul was impatient. "Here, let me do it!" he ordered, and he made the sacrifice himself.

At that moment Samuel arrived. "What have you done!" he cried. But Samuel could see that Saul had disobeyed God's law.

Saul began to make excuses instead of being sorry. "Foolish Saul," replied Samuel, "God made you king, not priest.

You have disobeyed him. Nothing is
worse in God's sight than to disobey God.

"God is to be first in this nation. Not
even the king is before him. You have
decided your way is better than his. You
have pretended to worship him this day.
But what you have really done is put
yourself before God. You have forgotten
the kind of king you promised to be when
God chose you.

"God was going to make your family

kings forever. Now he will find the kind of king he can trust."

And with those words, Samuel left Saul and went sadly home to Ramah.

Saul went on being king. He won many battles but got further and further away from God and his way. He was never willing to wait to find out what God wanted.

Finally, Saul failed another test. Just before a big battle, God sent Samuel to Saul with a message: "Take no prisoners. Don't save anything—animals, food, or other treasures."

But Saul took one prisoner—the wicked king. He also saved the best of the sheep and oxen. And he was so proud that he put up a monument to honor himself.

In the middle of the night, God told Samuel what Saul had done. The next day when Samuel came to Saul, the king lied, "I have done what God said."

"Then," said Samuel, "why do I hear sheep bleating and cows lowing?"

"The people did it to bring an offering

37

to God," was Saul's excuse.

"Stop! Hear what God has told me in the night." And Samuel gave the king bad news. "God would rather have you obey him than have you give many offerings. You have decided you know better than God. You have turned away from God, and he will turn away from you!"

Suddenly, Saul was afraid. He begged Samuel: "Forgive me. I did wrong, but only because I was afraid of what others would say. Don't leave me! Let's go worship together and everything will be all right."

But Samuel refused and turned to go. Saul tried to hold on to his robe and it tore. "That's what is happening to you, Saul," the prophet said. "God is tearing your kingdom away. He is giving it to someone who will listen to him and do what he says."

Once again Samuel went home to Ramah. He had loved Saul and tried to help him. Samuel was sad the rest of his life whenever he thought of how Saul had refused to be the kind of king God wanted.

Thinkback: What kind of king was Saul at first? What was the main advice God's prophet Samuel kept giving the king?

What two tests did the king fail? What was the main reason Saul did not please God?

An Old Prophet and a New King

Samuel was disappointed. He had hoped Saul would be the kind of king God's people needed. But Saul got worse and worse. And Samuel was sadder and sadder.

Then one day the old prophet heard God speak. "Samuel," God said, "why do you keep being sad? I have a new job for you. Get some olive oil and go to Bethlehem. Look for a farmer named Jesse. I have chosen one of his sons to be the next king."

Samuel was surprised. "How dare I! If Saul hears about it, won't he kill me?"

But God said: "I will tell you what to do. Just follow my orders, and you will be safe."

Samuel did what God asked. He took a

calf with him to make a sacrifice.

Samuel told the people in Bethlehem: "I come in peace. Get ready and worship God with me." The old prophet invited Jesse and his sons to the sacrifice, too.

A special time came. The sacrifice had not yet begun. Samuel noticed one of Jesse's sons. He was tall and handsome. Samuel thought, "This must surely be the one God wants to be the next king." But Samuel was wrong.

41

"I do not choose a person the way people do," God told Samuel. "People go by what a person looks like. I look at a person's heart. What someone thinks and believes is more important than looks and clothes."

And so, one by one, Jesse's seven sons came before Samuel. And, one by one, all were turned aside.

"Are these all your sons?" he asked.

"No, there is the youngest. He is a mere boy; he is caring for the sheep."

"Get him," Samuel said. "We shall not begin until he comes." And so they waited until young David came. He was healthy and handsome, and his eyes sparkled.

Samuel could tell this young man was special. Samuel again heard God speak: "This is the one. Anoint him!"

Samuel obeyed. He took out the oil he

43

had brought. It was in an animal's horn. There in private, with only his family watching, David knelt before Samuel.

Samuel was now very old. He had spent his whole life trying to help his people follow God. He had been disappointed many times, but he never gave up. Here before him was God's choice for king. Samuel knew that God was right. It was a very serious moment.

Slowly, Samuel anointed the young shepherd's head with the golden oil.

It would be many months, even years, before young David could be king. Saul would do all he could to keep that from happening. But, Samuel knew—and so did David—that God would be with David from that day on. And one day Israel would have a great, good king.

Back to Ramah Samuel went once more, probably to teach in his school. He had been a good judge, serving all the people fairly. He had been a wise leader in time of trouble. He had been God's preacher, reminding people what God

45

expected and helping them worship.

Samuel had many hard choices to make. But each time he tried to listen to what God wanted. He had to take second place more than once—and did it without grumbling. Right up to the end of his life, Samuel was willing to help others. He was busy doing whatever he felt God wanted, even when he did not know exactly why.

When Samuel died, people came from all over the land to honor him. And they buried his body at his home in Ramah.

Thinkback: What was alike and different about the way Saul and David were chosen to be king? Was Samuel famous? Why?

Reflections

● Hannah made a promise to give her child to God. Was that an easy promise to keep? What do you do when you have made a promise that is hard to keep?

● How is your place of worship alike and different from the place of worship where Samuel lived as a boy?

● God started speaking to Samuel when he was only a boy. Does God speak to boys and girls today? If so, how?

● What do you think was the hardest choice Samuel ever had to make? Why? What is the hardest choice you have made?

● Think of every word you can that describes Samuel. Use each one in a sentence like this: I know Samuel was ____ because _____ .

Then use the same word in another sentence: I can be ____ by _____ .